By Jan Glaesel

The Complete Method For Trumpet

IMPROVE YOUR GAME

COMPLETE EDITION VOLUME I-IV

Volume I-IV

VOLUME I - PAGE 21
WARM-UPS / INTERVAL & SLURRING EXERCISES

VOLUME II - PAGE 96
PEDAL TONES & LOW NOTES / 10 DAILY ROUTINES

VOLUME III - PAGE 176
ALL SCALES / TRANSPOSITION / DEXTERITY

VOLUME IV - PAGE 284
PERFORMANCE / TONGUING & TARGET / PRECISION & ENDURANCE / MUSICAL TREATS

WRITTEN BY: JAN GLAESEL
COPYRIGHT © 2012:
JAN GLAESEL / JGMUSIK APS DK
WWW.TRUMPETGAME.COM

INDEX - VOLUME I

Exercise	Page
Title Page Volume I	1
Index Volume I to IV	2-5
Foreword	6
How to use this book	10
Introduction To Chapters Vol. I	9
Introduction To Chapters Vol. II	16
Introduction To Chapters Vol. III	19
Warm-Ups	21
My Personal warm-up	21
The Gorrie warm-up	28
Does everything work? warm-up	30
Alternative warm-up	37
Interval cadenza warm-up	31
Scale "singing"	42
Wider scale "singing"	44
The lip bender warm-up	46
Flexibility warm-up	48
Legato power warm-up	53
Danish Folk Song	56
Wise Trumpet Tapas	57
Interval & Slurring Exercises	58
Interval studies major	58
Interval studies minor	60
Interval studies augmented (#5)	62
Interval studies major, minor, aug#5	64
Expanding flexi-slur studies	68
Expanding flexi, 1/2 notes	68
Wise Trumpet Tapas	71
Expanding flexi, 1/4 notes	72
Expanding flexi, 1/8 notes	74
Expanding flexi, 1/16 notes	76
Arban inspired Slur/Flexi Study	78
Interval range study	81
Octave Studies	86
Octave studies - Intro	86
Octave studies	87
Octave legato studies	90
Wise Trumpet Tapas	93-94

INDEX - VOLUME II

Exercise	Page
Pedal-Tones & Low Notes	96
Introduction to Chapters - Volume II	16
Introduction to pedal-tones	96
Pedaltones	97
Daily Routines - Week By Week	100
Daily Routine - Week 01	100
Daily Slurs - Week 01	103
Daily Routine - Week 02	106
Daily Slurs - Week 02	110
Daily Routine - Week 03	112
Daily Slurs - Week 03	116
Daily Routine - Week 04	118
Daily Slurs - Week 04	123
Daily Routine - Week 05	125

Exercise	Page
Daily Slurs - Week 05	129
Daily Endurance Part I - Week 06	132
Daily Endurance Part II - Week 06	135
Daily Routine - Week 07	137
Daily Slurs - Week 07	142
Daily Expanding Scales - Week 07	146
Daily Routine - Week 08	148
Daily Slurs - Week 08	153
Daily Routine - Week 09	157
Daily Slurs I - Week 09	162
Daily Slurs II - Week 09	163
Daily Routine - Week 10	165
Daily Slurs - Week 10	171
Wise Trumpet Tapas	174

INDEX - VOLUME III

Exercise	Page
Introduction to chapters - Volume III	19
The 12 Mixolydian Scales	220
All Scales	176
Major Scales & Triads	176
Minor Scales & Triads	178
The 12 Major Scales	180
The 12 Natural Minor Scales	182
The 12 Mel. Minor Scales	184
The 12 Harm. Minor Scales	186
Chromatic Scales I	188
Chromatic Scales II	191
Chromatic Scales III	193
Chromatic Scales IV	196
Moving Chromatic Scales	198
The Seven Modes	203
The Seven Modes Introduction	203
The 12 Ionian Scales	204
The 12 Dorian Scales	208
The 12 Phrygian Scales	212
The 12 Lydian Scales	216
The 12 Aeolian Scales	224
The 12 Locrian Scales	228
Wise Trumpet Tapas	233
Octatonic & Wholetone	234
First Octatonic Scales	234
Second Octatonic Scales	239
The 12 Wholetone Scales	244
Glaesels Brainboilers	248
Glaesels Brainboilers - Major	248
Glaesels Brainboilers - Minor	251
Glaesels Brainboilers - 1/1 tone	254
2 Alternativ Brainboiler Themes	257
Dexterity Studies	258
Dexterity Studies - Level I	258
Dexterity Studies - Level II	267
Dexterity Studies - Level III	277
Wise Trumpet Tapas	282

INDEX - VOLUME IV

Exercise	Page
Performance	284
Introduction to Jon Gorrie	284
Just another day at the office	285
Wise Trumpet Tapas	297
Tonguing	298
Single Tonguing/Attack	298
Focus On Attack	302
Single Tonguing Etude	304
Double Tonguing Level I	305
Double Tonguing Etude 1	309
Double Tonguing Level II	310
Double Tonguing Etude 2	318
Wise Trumpet Tapas	319
Triple Tonguing Level I	320
Triple Tonguing Level II	322
Triple Tonguing Slapstick Etude	328
Precision & Endurance	330
Target Practice Level I	330
Target Practice Level II	333
Target Practice Level III	337
Becoming A Marksman Level I	339
Becoming A Marksman Level II	340
Get Rid Of The Terror Level I	341
Get Rid Of The Terror Level II & III	342
Wise Trumpet Tapas	398

Exercise	Page
Musical Treats - Collection	343
Lyrical Etude Level I	343-345
Lyrical Etude Level II	346-347
Waltz For Trumpet	348
My First Etude For Trumpet	349
Etude Picturesque - E minor	350
Single Tonguing Etude	352
Double Tonguing Etude 1	353
Trumpet Menuet Etude - D minor	354
Playful Trumpet Etude - A major	356
Etude For A Friend	358
Yearning For Home	360
Etude Ritmico Spiccato	362
Double Tonguing Etude 2	364
Triple Tonguing - Slapstick Etude	365
Etude For A Mentor	366
Latin Jazz Etude	368
Wise Trumpet Tapas	371
Etude Melancolico	372
Lyrical Interval Etude - McNab	374
Trumpet Incorporated - Score	376-385
Trumpet Incorporated - Parts (5 trpts)	386
My Bookshelf	396
Credits	397

FOREWORD:

This is actually the second time I'm writing this foreword. Right now I'm sitting at Starbucks in Central Pattaya, Thailand. I've just spent the last two weeks here in solitude in this wonderful country, away from home, work, phones and daily decisions, to finally finish my Trumpet Method Book "Improve Your Game – The Complete Method Book for Trumpet"

This project started in 2004, and the first time I wrote this foreword was in 2008 somewhere in the airspace between the U.S. and Denmark. I had been working in Las Vegas as a musical director for one of my Danish friends, a musical show genius, who wanted to try things out "over there". In my spare time, I collected all my notes on practising into one huge pile, and then thought, "That's it – the book is done". But boy was I wrong. When I got back home, I started looking at my "new book" – and it was a complete mess. It took me another four years to complete this project, inventing new systems and exercises to make the project come together. Now I have a complete overview of my material, have tried most of my ideas on myself, and now feel confident knowing that I have something of real value to pass on to my fellow trumpet players.

HERE IS MY STORY:

While playing drums at the age of 6 in the Tivoli Boys Guard in Copenhagen, I practised the trumpet, and 8 years old I got my spot in the marching band and just fell in love with the instrument. I spent 10 years in Tivoli and by the time I retired at 16 years of age, I was a semi-professional musician. I could sight-read music, follow a conductor, learned to be on time, and learned all of the other things that make you successful in the business. But suddenly, I was "unemployed".

In high school I joined some different bands playing all different kinds of music. In the beginning I had a huge problem: There was no music to read!!! My whole life I had played from written music, and now suddenly I had to just play something and improvise. I was completely lost for a while, but with time came the courage to jump without a parachute. It sounded awful, and other trumpet players would probably have been kicked out of the band (unless you had a van or a rehearsal room), but I had something else. Due to my training in The Tivoli

Boys Guard, I had the power and technique to play all the high stuff, and I could play for hours without getting tired. On top of that I knew my theory, and had a flair for composing and arranging. So, whenever somebody needed an arrangement or song – they knew who to call. I stayed in business and started getting a lot of work. In 1979 I had the fortune to be approached by the Big Band Guru Thad Jones, who at that time lived in Denmark wanted to form a Danish/American big band - Eclipse. For the next 3 years I learned everything about being a big band section-player. That was an experience of a lifetime.

To cut a long story short, I ended up as Musical Director on Danish National TV and was placed in charge of some of the biggest acts in the entertainment business in Denmark. I became known as the guy who could play trumpet with one hand, and conduct with the other – and actually I can. I formed my own company writing music for feature film and commercials – boy I've written a lot of those.

A day is only 24 hours – that's a fact. So with a schedule as busy as mine has been for the last 20 years, I of course had to cut some corners. Since practising didn't pay bills, and wasn't fun – I cut down on that. For many years I never practised. I just played, played and played, because I didn't have the time to invest.

THIS WAS THE WAY IT USED TO BE

After months of preparation, writing, rehearsing and just minutes before the first downbeat on the opening night of a show, I would ask the band: "Has anybody seen my horn?" I would find it, oil the valves and just give it a kick in the #¤%&, and would (barely) survive that first night. After a couple of shows it would get easier, and no one would suspect that I never practiced. The truth of the matter was that if you had given me a simple Danish Folksong and asked me to play it mezzopiano – I would have tanked completely.

THE CROSSROAD

By 2004, we had played thousands of shows during a 15 year period so we decided to take an indefinite break. This wasn't a big problem for me as I had all my writing, arranging and producing jobs. BUT – what about my beloved trumpet? Now I had two options:

SELL MY HORNS – OR – START TO PRACTICE!!

This book is the proof of my decision. The way back to falling in love with my instrument again has been long, frustrating, and hard, but above all – really, really rewarding.

THE FIRST DAY AT "WORK"

After making the decision to find out how good a trumpet player I could have been, I started to practice. I had promised myself to practice at least one hour a day, and that sounded within reach for me. Then I experienced the scariest moment in my professional life. I went to my studio, got out the trumpet and stared at it for a loooong time, not knowing what to play. I played some scales – enough to make an hour pass by. But when I looked at the clock, only 3 minutes had passed. I put down the horn, and gave up.

I've never been good at defeat, so the next day I found my very old copy of Arban's Complete Conservatory Method For Trumpet. The Arban had been the bible for me in the Tivoli Boys Guard. I knew my way around it, but it had been a long time since I looked at it. I put together a one hour program of exercises from the Arban book, and had a really hard time getting it together. On the negative side it soon occurred to me what a lousy technique I had, but on the positive side, I started to improve – fast. Nothing is more rewarding than when you put in the effort and start getting results.

At a lecture in Copenhagen, American Business Coach **Keith Cunningham** came with a statement that really was an eye-opener for me. He said:

> "IF YOU HAVE A TALENT, NO MATTER WHAT IT IS, AND SPEND 3 HOURS A DAY FOR 3 YEARS ON IMPROVING YOUR SKILLS, YOU WILL AFTER THOSE 3 YEARS BE IN THE TOP 100 IN YOUR FIELD - WORLDWIDE!!"

An average lifespan is roughly 700,000 hours and you only have to spend 3,285 hours of those to get in the top 100 worldwide. How easy is that!! OK – if you want to stay at the top 100 or get to #1, you have to put in a lot of additional hours – but you get the picture.

Since I restarted my practice career, I've studied a lot of books from great brass players, including Allen Vizzutti, Arturo Sandoval, Schlossberg, Clark, Herring, Stamp, Caruso, Claude Gordon – you name it. I also picked a lot of brains, met and played with some terrific trumpet players to get the material together that helped point me in the right direction, and I really want to share this research and material with you.

Let me get one thing straight:
I CAN'T PLAY EVERYTHING I WROTE IN THIS BOOK!!!!

If I only wrote exercises that I could play – I wouldn't learn anything. But I'm getting there: hour by hour, day by day, exercise by exercise. The day I can play everything in this book, I will write another. Here is a promise to you. If you can play the "Lyrical Interval Etude" that I wrote and dedicated to Mr. Malcolm McNab (in Vol. 4) I'll write a new one dedicated to you. (I can't play it – yet)

At age 54 I'm all fired up about playing and practicing my horn and I'm planning on improving my game for the next many years. I can't tell you when I'll stop – and as long as the horn sounds a little bit better every day I pick it up – I'll keep blowing.

JAN GLAESEL
Copenhagen, Denmark - 2012

HOW TO USE THIS BOOK

This book has been divided into 4 separate and independent volumes so that you can dig into specific areas instead of having to buy one large book just for one section, such as "The 10 Daily Routines" or "All Scales".

- Vol. I – Warm-ups, interval & Slurring Exercises
- Vol. II – Pedal-tones & Low Notes / The 10 Daily Routines
- Vol. III – All Scales / Transposition & Dexterity Studies
- Vol. IV – Tonguing / Target, Precision & Endurance /Performance / Melodies & Etudes

---

IMPORTANT!!

I've come up with three basic "rules" that apply to this book. They are:

1. REST ALMOST AS MUCH AS YOU PLAY

Practising can be harder than playing a gig. When I started this journey, I would practise one hour a day. My mistake was that I played for a full hour without resting at all. So when 60 minutes were up, I was done, and after a couple of weeks my lips were like two bricks. If you want to practice playing your horn for one hour – you should practice for two hours. Get the idea? Rest is important.

2. 3 STRIKES AND YOU'RE OUT!!

This needs explanation. When you look through the book you will probably be a little intimidated over all the high notes and tiring phrases – don't be. All exercises are written so that every trumpet player on an intermediate level can benefit from them – as long as they practice using this **"3 strikes and you're out"** rule.

Whenever you reach your current range limit – **give it three attempts, then stop.** The next day you can give it a shot again. In a few days, you will experience that what was once impossible, is now a walk in the park.

Exercises like this are divided into two or three sections. If I state, "Don't continue beyond this point if not within your range", stay within you range a couple of more days, and it will come. Remember: **"Good Things Come To Those Who Wait."** And HEY!! If the whole high note concept isn't something interesting to you, don't go there!! Simply skip those exercises, and let your normal high C be the top of your range. Remember:
"No note is so high, that it can't be played an octave or two down"!!

3. PUT AS MUCH MUSIC AS POSSIBLE INTO EVERYTHING YOU PLAY

Let's face it – 95% of these exercises are plain boring when you just look at them. But if you try to put as much music or feeling into them when playing, you can make them come to life. On top of that you should play everything with the most beautiful sound you can imagine. These two things together are essential for getting to the point where time just flies when you practice.

In the Chapter on **Performance in Vol. 4**, I will share with you hundreds of ideas that made sense to me about trumpet playing that I picked up around fellow trumpet players and the internet. I call this, "Spiritual Tapas". In this same section, a good friend and fellow trumpet player **Jon Gorrie** will give you an introduction to his book "Performing In The Zone" – a book all performers should read.

LAST RULES:
"TREAT YOURSELF TO SOME OF THE ETUDES IN THE BACK OF EACH VOLUME"
&
"TAKE A DAY OFF FROM TRUMPET PLAYING EVERY WEEK!!"
LET'S PRACTICE!!

INTRODUCTION TO SELECTED STUDIES VOLUME I

INTRODUCTION TO SELECTED STUDIES VOLUME 1

Universal Warm Up - my personal pg. 21 - 27
A good warm up is essential for all trumpet players. I know that it's boring, but once you get into the habit you'll get the hang of it. A good warm-up will set you back 25 to 30 minutes in most method books. In my universe that's too much. 10 - 15 minutes is enough for me to soften up my lips.
A good warm up is necessary, but don't get too dependent on it. You should always be able to pick up your horn and start playing. Believe me, in the real world you will have to be able to do exactly that.

EXERCISE 1 PG. 21

Purely to soften up your lips and to get the air flowing. The tempo is only for guidance. You should time it so you're completely empty of air after each phrase.

EXERCISE 2 - 5 PG. 21 - 27

This will open up your sound and tune in your tongue. When you understand the principle of the exercise, close the book and play it by heart. Not reading will change your focus to the result. Finish of with the cool down phrase and take a 10 minute break before continuing.

ALTERNATIVE WARM UP. PG. 29 - 33
EXERCISE 1-2 PG. 37 - 38.

These exercises are related. Exercise 2 is a mirrored version of exercise 1.
Each exercise should be played with a full sound. When you understand the principle, close the book and just play it. Use your brain and ears.

EXERCISE 3 INTERVAL CADENZA PG. 39 - 41

This exercise is written to start airflow. It's builds around a standard I-IV-V7 progression. Again, once you understand the exercise, close the book and just play. Once you think you've got it all down, set yourself back by playing the suggested articulations.

EXERCISE 4 SCALE-SINGING PG. 42 - 43

If your horn sounds and feels clogged, scale-singing will solve the problem. This exercise takes you to standard high C. All trumpet players should have that within their range.

EXERCISE 5-6 WIDER SCALE-SINGING PG. 44 - 45

Here it's very important to implement the idea of "3 strikes and you're out". Playing all the way through the exercise will take you up to G above high C. Play until you reach your limit. Give it 3 attempts and then STOP!!!!!
The next day, play from the beginning again and see you can pass that your previous limit. If you continue with this I promise you that you'll expand you register to where you want. Play a cool down phrase where ever you stop.

THE LIP BENDER WARM UP PG. 46 - 47
EXERCISE 1

The lip bender warm up gives you a lot of control and is very good for intonation. Play the same phrase twice: first time with the correct fingering, and secondly by just bending the notes with the lips. The exercise follows the circle of fifths so you change intervals all the time.

EXERCISE 2

Don't play this exercise until you have mastered exercise 1

FLEXI WARM UP PG. 48 - 52
EXERCISE 1 PG. 48

Your focus should be on the interval between the first two notes in this exercise. Try to make the transition between the two notes (an ascending octave) as clean as possible by avoiding small tones or clicks in between notes.

EXERCISE 2 PG. 48

The same thing, but mirrored.

EXERCISE 3 PG. 48

The same as exercise 1 but ascending. The last two staves should be played using the "3 strikes and you're out" principle.

EXERCISE 4 PG. 49

The same thing, but mirrored.

EXERCISE 5 - 8 PG. 50 - 52

Same principle with clean switches between notes. Breathe every four bars, and use the "3 strikes and you're out" regime . This is important. Play the cool down phrase after you finish.

LEGATO POWER WARM-UP PG. 53 - 55
EXERCISE 1 PG. 45

This is one of the exercises I would bring to a desert island. If you use this exercise correctly, it will improve both your sound and range. Don't overdo. Use the "3 strikes..." concept. Play the cool down variations of the exercise on pg.47 when after you've finished.

DANISH FOLKSONG PG. 56

This should be the final touch to every warm up you play, whether it's long or short. I suggest you play the Danish folk song "I skovens dybe stille ro" but you can choose other tunes if you like, such as "Yesterday" by the Beatles or "Fjariln vingad syns på Haga" (Swedish folksong) Find some of your own. Play it in 3 keys: C - F - Bb, and take a 30 second break in between. Play with a full sound and play the melody exactly as written - no valve-tricks to make up for the difficult intervals. Take a ten minute break before continuing.

INTERVAL STUDIES - MAJOR, MINOR & AUGMENTED EX 1-4 PG. 58 - 67

This exercise is quite simple and in four variations. Major, minor, augmented and a combo version. Please don't read it every time. Get the idea of the first couple of keys, and then think the rest. In that way you can focus a lot more on the purpose of the exercise. Please play with suggested dynamics to put as much music into the exercise as possible. Also play the suggested articulations for variation.

EXPANDING FLEXIBILITY-SLUR STUDIES EX. 1-7 PG. 68 - 77

These exercises are actually the same - the time just changes. Please use the directions for where to stop so that you don't overdo it. Focus on hitting the centre of pitch. Remember the "3 strikes and you're out" rule. It applies here more than anywhere. Do not continue with ex. 2 until you have mastered ex. 1 and so on.

ARBAN INSPIRED SLUR/FLEX STUDY EX. 6 -7 PG. 78 - 80

Try hitting the centre of the pitch in all intervals, and put as much music into the exercise as possible.

INTERVAL RANGE STUDY EX. 8 PG. 81

Focus on the expanding intervals and try to be precise. It's ok to slow down as the expansion increases, in order to get it right. Better safe than sorry. "3 strikes and you're out" applies here, so don't force it.

INTRODUCTION TO OCTAVE STUDIES AND OCTAVE STUDIES PG 86 - 89.

Read directions on page 78

OCTAVE LEGATO STUDY PG. 90

This exercise is filled with music. Focus on the octave jumps and play with a full open sound and have a constant air flow.

LET'S GET GOING - AND REMEMBER THESE WISE WORDS:

"EVERYBODY WANTS TO BE THE HERO BUT NO ONE WANTS TO SLAY THE DRAGON"
QUOTE: WYNTON MARSALIS

INTRODUCTION TO SELECTED CHAPTERS VOLUME II

INTRODUCTION TO PEDAL-TONES PAGE 96

Read carefully the "Introduction To Pedal-tones" on page 12.

PEDAL-TONES STUDIES PAGE 97

Ex.1 This exercise takes you chromatically down from your low C. From low F and down focus on hitting the pitches as clean as possible. Keep the same embouchure all the way.
Ex.2 Have focus on slurring the octaves as clean as possible. Try to keep the same embouchure all the way.
Ex.3 Now we expand with an extra octave. It's ok to slow it down so you really can focus on

10 DAILY ROUTINES - WEEK BY WEEK PAGE 100 - 173

OBS!! Before starting on the Daily Routines you should go through the Pedal Tones section

Together these 10 Daily Routine is a powerful tool to improvement. By Daily Routines I don't mean that you absolutely have to play one every single day - but as all trumpet players have, there are days where you don't know what to practise - here they come in real handy. And whenever you feel a little out of shape, for instance after a vacation, build a suitable program around them. BUT - first time you get into these Daily Routine, you should create a program for a longer period of time and have the pleasure of feeling the rapid improvement by using them.

Start of course with "Daily Routine - Week 1" and play that for a week or so, until you can play it all the way through and remember the "3 strikes" rule. When you are comfortable with this - move on to "Daily Routine - Week 2" and so on.

And by the way - I hate to read low pedal-tones in there right notation, so I use a lot of 8va basso notation for your convenience.

Here's a run through of the construction of the exercises.
Each Daily Routine consist of two main parts:

DAILY ROUTINE - PART 01.

A daily thematic expanding routine in three parts.
Ex.1 = Phrase A. - Ex.2 = Phrase A&B - Ex.3 = Phrase A,B&C
All thematic routines with one exception (Week 6) goes round the circle of 5th for variation and constant change in register.

DAILY ROUTINE - PART 02.

A daily slurring routine in 2 or 3 parts.

DIRECTIONS FOR THE INDIVIDUAL EXERCISES.
DAILY ROUTINE - WEEK 1,2,3,4 - 8 AND 10:

This is actually the basic layout of the whole concept of all the Daily Routines. Read it through without playing ,so you get the fundamentals of the exercises. if I write "Opt.8vb........" it optional. Tempos are only suggestions. After the Daily Slur exercises, end with playing the "cool down phrase" and remember to take a good break before continuing.

THE EXCEPTIONS:
DAILY ROUTINE - WEEK 5 - PAGE 125

This exercise focuses on jumping i octaves. Ex. 1 is just jumping one octave. Ex. 2 is jumping 2 octaves - one at a time going down. Ex.3 is also jumping 2 octaves, first 1 octave up - and then 2 down finishing of with a diminished appegio going up. The high endings are optional.

DAILY ROUTINE . WEEK 6 - ENDURANCE - PAGE 132

In this exercise it's crucial that you follow my rule number 2 :"3 strikes and you're out". Otherwise you'll hurt yourself, and that's definitely not the object of this exercise. The object is to strengthen your chops and the only way to do that, is NOT to overdo it. Whenever you hit the wall - give it 3 attempt - THEN STOP!! I promise you "Good things come to the ones that wait".

DAILY ROUTINE - WEEK 7 - PAGE 137

Actually it follows the basic layout of the rest of the routines, but it has a little bonus. After The Daily Slurs, there's a Expanding Major Scale exercise. It's a simple scale over a sixth stretching from G to E, next one expands in each end, from F# to F#, then F to G and so on. Last one expands from G below the system to double G. Again remember rule nr. 2: "3 strikes and you're out".

DAILY ROUTINE - WEEK 9 - PAGE 157

Same as Week 7 with and added bonus in the slur section. The slur exercises are not in intervals, but they're chromatic and expanding. Daily Slur I is over 2 octaves, and Daily Slur II is over 3 octaves. The expansion is only in one end - every version starts at G below the staff and expands with a semitone at the top. Remember - "3 strikes and you're out".

LET'S GET GOING - AND REMEMBER THESE WISE WORDS:

"YOU CAN'T HIRE SOMEONE TO PRACTISE FOR YOU"
QUOTE: H. JACKSON BROWN JR.

INTRODUCTION TO SELECTED CHAPTERS VOLUME III

ALL ABOUT SCALES - IMPROVE YOUR GAME VOLUME III

You can't be a trumpet player and work on a professional level without knowing something about scales. I used to only know the basics, but the last couple of years have inspired me to learn about all facets of trumpet technique, including scales. During my journey I had a hard time finding books for trumpet on the subject. I found a ton of books for piano and guitar, so I decided that I would dedicate a good portion of this book to scales, written so that they fit the range of the trumpet. Here we go.

THE MAJOR AND MINOR SCALES & THEIR TRIADS - PAGE. 176-177

These are absolute basics. I put it in just in case you forgot them. Both major and minor scales go around the circle of fifths.

THE 12 MAJOR & MINOR SCALES: ONE AND TWO OCTAVES - PAGE 180-187

Exactly as I write above the exercise, these are "not too interesting, but necessary".
You can choose to play these exercises in two ways. Either you can read them all the way through, or as I recommend, just read the first couple of keys and then use your brain to figure out the rest. That way, the scales will stick in your mind, and before you know it, all keys will be played naturally. Remember the "3 strikes and you're out" rule. This goes for all scale exercises.

CHROMATIC SCALE EXERCISES
ALL EXERCISES PG. 188-202

Chromatic scales are so easy to play on paper, but once you get into them you it's hard to see the forest for the trees. It's so easy to lose your bearings. "Where am I? How do I get down from here? What octave am I in?" These are all questions that can stop your flow, so start slowly. This is the best advice I can give you concerning chromatic scales.

THE SEVEN MODES OF THE DIATONIC MAJOR SCALE - PAGE 203-247
Please read introduction og page 203

GLAESELS BRAINBOILERS - MAJOR, MINOR AND WHOLE TONE - PAGE 248-256
These exercises are really good for your brain. I use them for practising transposition. It's always good to be able to move a phrase to another key, so this is the object of the exercise. Play the phrase in C and get it in your head. Again, here it's important to close your eyes and think the other keys once the phrase is in your mind. You may feel frustrated the first couple of days, but stay with it. It will pay off.

TWO ALTERNATIVE BRAINBOILER THEMES - PAGE 257
Once you know the original Brainboiler Theme inside out, you can start working on these two alternatives. I only wrote them in C, so here you HAVE to use your head to transpose them :)

DEXTERITY EXERCISES - LEVEL I, II & III - PAGE 258-281
"Repetition is the mother of skill" is a phrase that applies to many aspects of both music and trumpet playing. This exercise is inspired by Carmine Caruso's "Musical Calisthenics for Brass". I have just developed it further to include all other keys. The exercise should challenge you with repetitive fingerings that will develop your dexterity. My dexterity sucks because I'm left handed and I use my right hand on the valves. I have to practice complicated phrases a lot, so these exercises help me.

LET'S GET GOING - AND REMEMBER THESE WISE WORDS:
"HOW DO I GET TO CARNEGIE HALL? PRACTISE - PRACTISE - PRACTISE!! "
QUOTE: SAADI

NOTE!! :
INTRODUCTIONS TO CHAPTER FOR VOL IV - WRITTEN PRIOR TO EACH EXERCISE

My Personal
Universal Warm-Up
Please read "Introduction To Chapters" for reference - see index

Cool down phrase

Take a 10 mininute break

This warm up covers all areas

The Gorrie Warm Up

Finishing this book I met with my good friend, trumpet player and author of the book "Performing in the Zone" Jon Gorrie, and we played together for a couple of days in Gothenburg where he lives. I surgested that we played his warm up routine - getting a new warm up routine, once in a while is very inspiring.

The good thing about Jon warm-up is that it forces you to get your breathing going, and also covers the pedaltone area. If you're not familiar with pedaltones, please go to the pedaltone chapter in Vol II first. Every four bars should be palyed in one breath. If you don't fill up your lungs, you'll be screwed the lover you get.

Here is Jon's personal touch to the start of every key - so your starting point is the same.

© 2012 Improve Your Game - JGMusik ApS DK

Gentlemen - "Start your engines - the right way!!

Does everything work ? - Warm Up

On a regular basis, when time allows it, I meet with my good friend Nikolaj Viltoft, trumpetplayer at The Danish Royal Philharmonic, and we play for a couple of hours, drink coffee and finish of with a good lunch. We always exchange ideas, and last time he gave me this warm-up that kind of gives you a complete check-up on breathing and attack. The best aspect of this is that you mirror the exercise all the time - that forces you to stay focused.

I urge you to meet with fellow trumpet player once in a while to exchange ideas - it's so inspiring to find out, that what's hard for you, is exactly as hard for everybody else. Some times you feel that you're the only one with the problem. Guess what - You're NOT!!!

36

My second choice
Alternative Warm-Up
Please read "Introduction To Chapters" for reference - see index

Simile......................

Conclusion:

Don't read - use your brain
Interval Cadenza
Please read "Introduction To Chapters" for reference - see index

Scale-Singing

Open up your sound

Please read "Introduction To Chapters" for reference - see index

Wider Scale - "Singing"

Take a deeeeeeep breath!

Please read "Introduction To Chapters" for reference - see index

{Exercise 5 - sheet music in keys of G, A♭, A, B♭, B, C with "Your Choice" tempo, mf-f-mf dynamics, repeat 2-3 x}

Do not continue to Ex. #6 before mastering Ex. #5 without getting tired

Cool down phrase (*if stopping here - otherwise skip*)

Take a 10 minute break

© 2012 Improve Your Game - JGMusik ApS DK

Doesn't sound good - and it shouldn't
The Lip Bender Warm-Up
Please read "Introduction To Chapters" for reference - see index

♩ = **60** Use written fingering where indicated.

© 2012 Improve Your Game - JGMusik ApS DK

48

Be precise with the intervals

Flexibility Warm-Up

Please read "Introduction To Chapters" for reference - see index

Only if within your range - Remember: "*3 strikes and you're out!!*"

© 2012 Improve Your Game - JGMusik ApS DK

Only if within your range - Remember: "3 strikes and you're out!!"

After cool down phrase - take a 10 minute break before continuing

Cool down phrase

© 2012 Improve Your Game - JGMusik ApS DK

6

Only if within your range - Remember: "*3 strikes and you're out!!*"

After cool down phrase - take a 10 minute break before continuing

Cool down phrase

Legato Power Warm-Up

Please read "Introduction To Chapters" for reference - see index

You know the feeling. Some days it feels like someone left something inside your horn. The resistance feels crazy, but the problem is that your sound just hasn't opened up. The day after a tough gig can be one of those days. This exercise helps you open up your sound again. No key signatures - just all the "white keys" is the base of this exercise. This one is a no brainer - just focus on air and sound.

Play with an open and full sound, and think of each phrase as one long AAAAAAAHHHHHHHHH!

Play only within your range and with the principle: "*3 strikes and you're out!!*"

54

Don't end your warm-up without this!!
Danish Folk Song
Please read "Introduction To Chapters" for reference - see index

Tip: Blow freely with a full sound!!

Andante Cantabile

Wait 1-2 minutes before playing next version

Andante Cantabile

Wait 1-2 minutes before playing next version

Andante Cantabile

Cool down phrase

Take 10 minute break before continuing

© 2012 Improve Your Game - JGMusik ApS DK

WISE TRUMPET TAPAS - "PRACTISING"

Get "set" before you play your first note.

When seated, be ready to stand - When standing, be ready to run.

EVERYBODY WANTS TO BE THE HERO BUT NO ONE WANTS TO SLAY THE DRAGON
— WYNTON MARSALIS

Analysis is paralysis.

Know if you are a color or the lead

A section player must be selfless, willing to make the other players sound good by blending with them.

If your lyrical playing is strong, make your technical playing match it

Old habits do not disappear. New habits take the place of old. If you're lazy, old habits will take over.

Play with the most beautiful sound you can imagine

Take a day off each week - it's just trumpet playing!!

Don't read it - think and understand it

Interval Studies
Major, minor & Augmented

Please read "Introduction To Chapters" for reference - see index

Six suggestions for articulation

♩ = your choice (Remember - Nothing is so fast that it can't be played slower) :-)

Interval Studies - minor

Apply same articulations as in exercise 1
♩ = your choice

Interval Studies - Augmented (#5)

Apply same articulations as in exercise 1
♩ = your choice

© 2012 Improve Your Game - JGMusik ApS DK

Interval Studies - Major, minor & Augmented (#5)

Apply same articulations as in exercise 1
♩ = your choice

Take a 10 minute break

Boring - but rewarding

Expanding Flexibility-Slur Study - Half Notes

Please read "Introduction To Chapters" for reference - see index

Alternative articulations:

Stop here and play the cool down phrase if the rest of exercise is not within your range.

Cool down phrase

Take A Ten Minute Break

Play only if within your range. Remember - "*3 strikes and you're out*"

Simile.......

WISE TRUMPET TAPAS - "PRACTISE"

- Practise pianissimo

- **CONSIDER DEVOTING LESS TIME TO REPETITIVE MATERIAL, AND MORE TIME DOING MUSICAL MATERIAL**

- Assign yourself material and stay with it daily for a specific number of days (6 to 10)

- Practise playing on cold chops in order to be ready for any situation

- Always incorporate music into your warm up.

- Do something else to fill the space while you are resting - internet for instance :-)

- Rest as much as you play.

- Practise with a friend!!

- Use pedal tones and a 10-20 min. rest to extend your practise.

- Set small realistic goals for yourself - every day

Better slow and precise than fast and sloppy

Expanding Flexibility-Slur Study - Quarter Notes

Please read "Introduction To Chapters" for reference - see index

Stop here and play the cool down phrase if the rest of the exercise is not within your range - otherwise continue

73

Cool down phrase

Take A Ten Minute Break

Play only if within your range

After Cool Down Phrase - Take A Ten Minute Break

Cool down phrase

75

Cool down phrase

Take A Ten Minute Break

Play only if within your range

Simile.......

Simile.......

Simile.......

Simile.......

Cool down phrase

Take A Ten Minute Break

Expanding Flexibility-Study - Sixteenth Notes

If you think this is easy - think again!

Please read "Introduction To Chapters" for reference - see index

I grew up on Arban - I owe him a lot!!
Arban-inspired Slur/Flexibility Study
Please read "Introduction To Chapters" for reference - see index

I promise - we're done soon!!

Interval Range Study

Please read "Introduction To Chapters" for reference - see index

Alternative articulations

84

Cool down phrase

Take A Ten Minute Break

Introduction To Octave Studies

These next octave studies are extremely difficult – but necessary. There are several purposes, but the most important is to improve your accuracy. If you showed up to a gig and were presented with music with phrases like the ones you're about to play, you would say that they were not written for trumpet. Well, they are not.
BUT – if you can master them your accuracy rate will improve drastically.

To be accurate while descending is as difficult as being accurate ascending - and just as important. Exercises 3 and 4 focus on descending. Here are a couple of tips for playing both exercises:

To avoid hitting wrong notes you often develop the bad habit of under-blowing high notes, while compensating with increased muscle tension. Forget that and back your intentions up <u>WITH AIR</u>. That will solve the problem and give you great confidence. Only play exercises 2 and 4 after you have mastered exercises 1 and 3.
Don't overdo it - that would be counterproductive..

© 2012 Improve Your Game - JGMusik ApS DK

Ready..... Aim..... Fire!!

Octave Studies

(Please read introduction on previous page)

Remember - "*3 strikes and you're out!*"

Simile......

Octave Legato Study
(Please read introduction to chapter for reference)

WISE TRUMPET TAPAS – "THE INSTRUMENT"

Don't mistake volume for intensity

Ease mouthpiece pressure at all rests and phrase endings

SLAM THE VALVES. JUST THROW THE BALL – DON'T THINK!!

Make your primary instrument the Bb trumpet. C trumpet makes you tight.

When choosing a mouthpiece, consider having somebody listen to you from across the room

Mouthpiece: The best solutions come from retaining the cup, throat and rim and changing the backbore.

Do not owerblow!!

ON C TRUMPET, ALWAYS USE 23 FOR EB AND 12 FOR E – DO NOT USE 13 FOR D OR HIGH G

Practise piccolo parts on Bb trumpet.

Know when to use alternate fingerings and when they are not needed.

Sing!

WISE TRUMPET TAPAS - "BREATHING"

- Do not owerblow!!
- **DON'T FORCE THE AIR**
- **DON'T HOLD BACK THE AIR.**
- Use the nosebreath to avoid unseating the embouchure
- Accelerate the air when ascending - decelerate the air when descending.
- It's important to blow freely, so as not to crush the lips and pinch the tone
- Breathe as though you were going to swim underwater to the other side of the pool.
- Use slow breathing - in through the nose and out through the mouth - to counteract performance anxiety.
- **Breathe up until the point of playing.**
- On a scale from 1-10, take a "10" breath every time
- Fill your lungs from the bottom and use them as a bellows
- Blow through the notes

By Jan Glaesel
The Complete Method For Trumpet

IMPROVE YOUR GAME

PEDAL-TONE STUDIES & 10 DAILY ROUTINES

Volume II

WRITTEN BY: JAN GLAESEL
COPYRIGHT © 2012:
JAN GLAESEL / JGMUSIK APS DK
WWW.TRUMPETGAME.COM

The secret to high notes? Go through the low notes

Introduction To Pedal-tones

What are pedal-tones and what purpose do they serve? If you look at the example above you can see many low notes extending below the normal range of the trumpet. Why are they called pedal-tones? They derived their name from the low notes played with the feet on an organ.

From middle C to low F# are actual tones within the trumpet's range.
But from low F to Db, I refer to them as "False Pedal-tones". Here is the explanation.

By pressing the valves, in various combinations, there are 7 different tones in the harmonic series descending from middle C to low F#.

1. valve lower the pitch with a whole tone
2. valve lower the pitch with a semi-tone
3. valve lower the pitch with a whole tone + a semi-tone

In various combinations, the valves gives you the seven different fundamental pitches in the harmonic series. When you go from your lowest actual note on the horn, low F#, to F, you go from a fundamental pitch to the first false pedal tone F. Why is it false? Well, it's because it belongs to the fundamental pitch Bb, so you have to "lip" the note down to get the right pitch. If you continue down, you have to do this all the way to pedal C where you again hit a fundamental pitch.

If you want to recieve all the benefits from playing pedal-tones it's crucial that you play all true fundamental pitches as such, and with the correct fingering. For some, it's easier to play pedal-tones with false fingerings. Played in this manner, you do not receive all the benefits of playing it correctly. So continuing down from pedal C, play as fundamental pitches and use correct fingerings.

Pedal-tones are supposed to sound awful, so don't get frustrated and don't over-do it!!

I despise reading low notes. All those ledger lines! Very frustrating! So throughout this chapter,
I will always notate as indicated in the example below:

© 2012 Improve Your Game - JGMusik ApS DK

It's messy in the beginning
Pedal-tones Studies

Try to play this chromatic scale with a good sound and as evenly as possible.

Now you get the idea with the false pedals, so I'll stop marking the fingerings.

Rest Your Chops Before Continuing!

Daily Slurs - Week 01

Take a 5-10 minute break before continuing.

While resting, keep the energy flowing.
Do something productive!

Daily Routine - Week 02

(Please read "Introduction to chapters" for reference - see index)

108

Rest 5-10 minutes before continuing.
Have a cup of coffee or surf the internet.

Daily Slur - Week 02

By now you're probably gettin' the hang of it.

Daily Routine - Week 03

(Please read "Introduction to chapters" for reference - see index)

Rest 5-10 minutes before continuing.
What about a little time on twitter?

Daily Slurs - Week 03

Daily Routine - Week 04

Don't read - think!!

(Please read "Introduction to chapters" for reference - see index)

© 2012 Improve Your Game - JGMusik ApS DK

Daily Slurs - Week 04

Now we're cranking it up a notch!
Daily Routine - Week 05
(Please read "Introduction to chapters" for reference - see index)

Take a 5-10 min break before continuing. Have a cup of coffee.

Daily Slurs - Week 05

Take a 5-10 minute break before continuing. Hug the wife or pet the dog. Or both! :)

What does'nt kill you - makes you stronger

Daily Routine - Week 06 - Endurance Part I

(Please read "Introduction to chapters" for reference - see index)

Rest as needed between each key.

From here on, there are no more pedal-tones. That's why every key ends with tonic - 5th - tonic.

Take a 10-15 minute break and something that has nothing to do with playing the trumpet

Daily Routine - Week 06 - Endurance - Part II

Rest as needed between each key.

You can continue higher if you want. I'm happy with my high G.   :-)

Finally - soften your lips with this exercise

Rest for at least 20 minutes before contnuing. Have a cup of coffee. Good job!!!

Still not cracking walnuts with your lips? Don't worry - you will!!!

Daily Routine - Week 07

(Please read "Introduction to chapters" for reference - see index)

© 2012 Improve Your Game - JGMusik ApS DK

140

Daily Slurs - Week 07

This is Macho!!

Daily Routine - Week 07 - Expanding Major Scales

(Please read "Introduction to chapters" for reference - see index)

© 2012 Improve Your Game - JGMusik ApS DK

Rest 5-10 minutes before continuing.

Rest 10 to 15 minutes before continuing.

Daily Slurs - Week 08

© 2012 Improve Your Game - JGMusik ApS DK

Now it's really getin' tough
Daily Routine - Week 09
(Please read "Introduction to chapters" for reference - see index)

158

Rest 10 to 15 minutes before continuing. The end is near!!!

Daily Slurs 1 - Week 09
Expanding Chromatic Scales - Two Octaves

Daily Slurs 2 - Week 09
Expanding Chromatic Scales - Three Octaves

After this - you're done!!

Daily Routine - Week 10

(Please read "Introduction to chapters" for reference - see index)

Rest 10 to 15 minutes before continuing. Good job!!

When you're done with this - you're through!

Daily Slurs - Week 10
Octave intervals using leading notes - Level I

Simile.......

Simile.......

Simile.......

Simile.......

Simile.......

© 2012 Improve Your Game - JGMusik ApS DK

Octave intervals using leading notes - Level II

Simile.......

Simile.......

Simile.......

Simile.......

Simile.......

© 2012 Improve Your Game - JGMusik ApS DK

Octave intervals using leading notes - Level III

Simile.......

Simile.......

Simile.......

Simile.......

Cool down phrase

Rest 5-10 minutes before continuing. Maintain you profile on Facebook

© 2012 Improve Your Game - JGMusik ApS DK

WISE TRUMPET TAPAS - "PRACTISE"

- Practise Slowly

- Practise what troubles you, not what you already can do.

- **INTEGRATE TECHNIQUE** IT MUST SERVE A MUSICAL END. **PRACTISE** IS NOT OUR SOLE PURPOSE. **MUSICAL** PERFORMANCE IS THE GOAL.

- If you practise nothing else that day, be sure to follow the routine with at least a lyrical study.

- When practising – always perform.

- Strive for 20 out of 20 times accuracy when practising a passage.

- You play the way you practise.

- Practise with a friend!!

- Make a list of your weaknesses and get to work on them.

- Every note you play must be musical!!

By Jan Glaesel

The Complete Method For Trumpet

IMPROVE YOUR GAME

ALL SCALES TRANSPOSITION & DEXTERITY STUDIES

Volume III

WRITTEN BY: JAN GLAESEL
COPYRIGHT © 2012:
JAN GLAESEL / JGMUSIK APS DK
WWW.TRUMPETGAME.COM

The Major Scales and Their Triads-Sharp Keys

Just in case you forgot!!

Please read "Introduction to chapters" for reference - see index

Clock-wise round the circle of 5ths.

The Major Scales and Their Triads-Flat Keys

Counter-clockwise round the circle of 5ths.

Just in case you forgot these talso!!

The Minor Scales & Their Triads-Sharp Keys

Clock-wise round the circle of 5ths.

The Minor Scales & Their Triads-Flat Keys

Counter-clockwise round the circle of 5ths.

Not too interesting - but necessary

The 12 Major Scales - One Octave

Please read "Introduction to chapters" for reference - see index

The 12 Major Scales - Two Octaves

© 2012 Improve Your Game - JGMusik ApS DK

Try not to read it - think it instead.

The 12 Natural minor Scales - One Octave

The 12 Natural minor Scales - Two Octaves

It's gettin' tougher.......

The 12 Melodic minor Scales - One Octave

minor scale with raised 6th and 7th degree ascending, lowered while descending

The 12 Melodic minor scales - Two Octaves

minor scale with raised 6th and 7th degree ascending, lowered while descending

Sounding a bit Middle Eastern.....

The 12 Harmonic Minor scales - One octave

minor scale with raised 7th degree - both ascending and descending

The 12 Melodic minor Scales - Two Octaves

minor scale with raised 7th degree -both ascending and descending

© 2012 Improve Your Game - JGMusik ApS DK

This will mess your brain up

Chromatic Exercise 1 - One Octave
Please read "Introduction to chapters" for reference - see index

Middle Register

♩ = your choice for all exercises

Chromatic Exercise 2 - Triplets, One & 1/2 Octave

Middle Register

Chromatic Exercise 3 - One Octave In Circle of 5ths

Middle Register

Chromatic Exercise 4 - Two Octaves, Chromatic

Moving Chromatic Studies

Alternative articulations exercise 1-4

♩ = your choice

Alternative articulations exercise 5-7

Play only if within your range

The Seven Modes of the Diatonic Major Scale

The next topic is HUGE!! I hate it myself, but as an old trumpet player friend told me that if you can't do anything else, you MUST know all scales and keys and play them effortlessly.

When I played in the Tivoli Boys Guard, we were taught all the normal Major and minor scales. But when I set out as a commercial player, I was introduced to the following old-fashioned names used in modern music: **Ionan, Dorian Phrygian, Lydian, Mixolydian, Aeolian and Locrian.**

To me, they sounded like characters from "Lord of the Rings". I hated the names so much that I didn't bother to learn them. Since turning 50, I've become a sucker for learning and have added these scales in my musical vocabulary. Here is a mnemonic phrase that I use to help remember the names of these scales:

I Don't **P**lay **L**ike **M**r. **A**rmstrong **L**ately

Note that the first letters of each word are the first letters of each scale. Pretty cool, huh? Try to come up with your own mnemonic phrase to help you remember these scales. Be creative!

Below is a breakdown of the seven modes. Take a "normal" C major scale (all the white keys on the piano from C to C). Now move it one whole step and play it from D to D. Now you have a Dorian D scale. It's a Dm scale that fits Dm6, m7 & 13 chord. At first look at the charts, but as soon as you understand it - close the book and use your head instead.

These next exercises are dedicated to these scales in all 12 keys.

© 2012 Improve Your Game - JGMusik ApS DK

Here we go - but this one is easy

The 12 Ionian Scales - One Octave

Major scale with raised 7th degree - associated with maj7 chords

1x: Slured
2x: Tenuto
3x: Staccato

Simile...

Simile...

Simile...

Simile...

Simile...

© 2012 Improve Your Game - JGMusik ApS DK

F#

Simile...

G

Simile...

A♭

Simile...

A

Simile...

B♭

Simile...

B

Simile...

The 12 Ionian Scales - Two Octaves
Major scale with raised 7th degree - associated with maj7 chords

1x: Slured
2x: Tenuto

C

Db

Simile...

D

Simile...

Eb

Simile...

E

Simile...

F

Simile...

© 2012 Improve Your Game - JGMusik ApS DK

The 12 Dorian Scales - One Octave

1x: Slured
2x: Tenuto
3x: Staccato

minor scale with low 7th degree - associated with minor 6,7 and 13 chords

© 2012 Improve Your Game - JGMusik ApS DK

F#
Simile.......

G
Simile.......

Ab
Simile.......

A
Simile.......

Bb
Simile.......

B
Simile.......

© 2012 Improve Your Game - JGMusik ApS DK

The 12 Dorian Scales - Two Octaves

minor scale with low 7th degree - associated with minor 6,7 and 13 chords

1x: Slured
2x: Tenuto

© 2012 Improve Your Game - JGMusik ApS DK

© 2012 Improve Your Game - JGMusik ApS DK

The 12 Phrygian Scales - One Octave

1x: Slured
2x: Tenuto
3x: Staccato

minor scale with lowered 2nd, 6th and 7th degree - associated with sus4 and b9 chords

© 2012 Improve Your Game - JGMusik ApS DK

Simile.......

Simile.......

Simile.......

Simile.......

Simile.......

The 12 Phrygian Scales - Two Octaves

minor scale with lowered 2nd, 6th and 7th degree - associated with sus4 and b9 chords

1x: Slured
2x: Tenuto

© 2012 Improve Your Game - JGMusik ApS DK

F# Phrygian

G Phrygian

G# Phrygian

A Phrygian

Bb Phrygian

B Phrygian

The 12 Lydian Scales - One Octave

Major scale with raised 4th and 7th degree - associated with maj7, #11 chords

1x: Slured
2x: Tenuto
3x: Staccato

© 2012 Improve Your Game - JGMusik ApS DK

The 12 Lydian Scales - Two Octaves

Major scale with raised 4th and 7th degree - associated with maj7, #11 chords

1x: Slured
2x: Tenuto

© 2012 Improve Your Game - JGMusik ApS DK

The 12 Mixolydian Scales - One Octave

Minor scale with lowered 7th degree

1x: Slured
2x: Tenuto
3x: Staccato

© 2012 Improve Your Game - JGMusik ApS DK

Simile...

Simile...

Simile...

Simile...

Simile...

Simile...

The 12 Mixolydian Scales - Two Octaves

Minor scale with lowered 7th degree

1x: Slured
2x: Tenuto

© 2012 Improve Your Game - JGMusik ApS DK

The 12 Aeolian Scales - One Octave

minor scale with lowered 6th and 7th degree- associated with m7, b13 chords

1x: Slured
2x: Tenuto
3x: Staccato

simile...

simile...

simile...

simile...

simile...

simile...

The 12 Aeolian Scales - Two Octaves

minor scale with lowered 6th and 7th degree- associated with m7, b13 chords

1x: Slured
2x: Tenuto

simile...

simile...

simile...

simile...

simile...

© 2012 Improve Your Game - JGMusik ApS DK

The 12 Locrian Scales - One Octave

minor scale with low 2nd, 5th, 6th and 7th step - associated with m7, b5 chords

1x: Slured
2x: Tenuto
3x: Staccato

simile...

simile...

simile...

simile...

simile...

© 2012 Improve Your Game - JGMusik ApS DK

simile...

simile...

simile...

simile...

simile...

simile...

232

That's it!!! - You're through - BUT!!!!!!!!!..........

© 2012 Improve Your Game - JGMusik ApS DK

WISE TRUMPET TAPAS - "FUNNY"

How do trumpet players traditionally greet each other?

"Hi . Nice to meet you. I'm better than you."

Four trumpet players are in a minivan. The minivan goes off a cliff. What's the tragedy in this? You can fit 8 trumpet players in a minivan.

How do you improve the aerodynamics of a trumpet player's car? Take the Domino's Pizza sign off the roof.

Why does a trumpet have three valve? Because trumpet players can't count to four!!

Why can't a gorilla play trumpet? It's too sensitive.

What's the difference between trumpet players and government bonds? Government bonds eventually mature and earn money.

What's the difference between a trumpet and a chain saw? Vibrato, though you can minimize this difference by holding the chain saw very still.

What is a gentleman? Somebody who knows how to play trumpet - but doesn't

When in doubt, add a shake!!

First 12 Octatonic Scales - One Octave

Diminished scale (half step-whole step) - associated with diminished chords

1x: Slured
2x: Tenuto
3x: Staccato

© 2012 Improve Your Game - JGMusik ApS DK

First 12 Octatonic Scales - Two Octaves

Diminished scale (half step-whole step) - associated with diminished chords

Second 12 Octatonic Scales - One Octave

Diminished scale (whole step-half step) - associated with diminished chords

1x: Slured
2x: Tenuto
3x: Staccato

F#

simile...

G

simile...

Ab

simile...

A

simile...

Bb

simile...

B

simile...

Second 12 Octatonic Scales - Two Octaves

1x: Slured
2x: Tenuto

Diminished scale (whole step-half step) - associated with diminished chords

simile...

simile...

simile...

© 2012 Improve Your Game - JGMusik ApS DK

The 12 Wholetone Scales - One Octave

(whole-tone-whole-tone) - associated with dominant 7#5 chords

1x: Slured
2x: Tenuto
3x: Staccato

© 2012 Improve Your Game - JGMusik ApS DK

F#

simile...

G

simile...

Ab

simile...

A

simile...

Bb

simile...

B

simile...

The 12 Wholetone Scales - Two Octave

(whole-tone-whole-tone) - associated with dominant 7#5 chords

1x: Slured
2x: Tenuto

© 2012 Improve Your Game - JGMusik ApS DK

simile...

simile...

Soften your embouchure by playing these low versions

simile...

simile...

simile...

simile...

simile...

simile...

simile...

Soften you embrochure by playing these low versions

simile...

simile...

simile...

simile...

simile...

Let's get dizzy!!

Glaesel "Brainboiler" - Whole-note

E

F

Soften your embouchure by playing these low versions

B

B♭

A

A♭

G

© 2012 Improve Your Game - JGMusik ApS DK

Here is the sketch - you finish the drawing!!

Two Alternative "Brainboiler" Themes

Please read "Introduction to chapters" for reference - see index

*Note - Diminished version not possible.

© 2012 Improve Your Game - JGMusik ApS DK

Repetition is the mother of skill

Dexterity Exercises - Level 1

Please read also "Introduction to chapters" for reference - see index

This exercise looks looooooong and boring. Well, you know what? It is!!! But the scary part is actually finding out how difficult it is simply to repeat a sequence of fingerings - over and over again. This exercise strenghtens your dexterity as well as improving your stamina.

We start with 1/8-note triplets, proceed to 1/16-notes , and then on from there. I only write up to a quintuplet, but you can expand rhythmically if you're into it. Go for it!!!

In Exercise 14 we expand to two octaves. Remember - if you don't get it in 3 strikes - you're out. Eventually you will succeed - I promise!

Do yourself a favor. Thoroughly understand the concept of each exercise. Then close the book (and your eyes) and focus on your fingers. If you have to read all exercises, this chapter will be a pain in the "@#*%#@"!

Spread the different rhythms out over your week or just take 2-3 each day so you don't get crazy. 1/8-note triplets on Monday, 1/16-notes on Tuesday, etc..

TIP!! To get the most out of these exercises, "bang" the valves down so shifting between notes becomes as distinct as possible.

© 2012 Improve Your Game - JGMusik ApS DK

260

Expanding to two octaves. Remember - *3 strikes and you're out!!*

Take a nice long break and play something meaningful.

I'll have you committed to this before Level 3
Dexterity Exercises - Level 2

It still looks looooong and boring - and it still is. We started with 1/8-note triplets so now we go on to 1/16 notes.

In Exercise 14 we go again expand to two octaves. Remember again - if you don't get it in three attempts - you're out. Eventually you will succeed - I promise!!

Do yourself a favor. Thoroughly understand the concept of each exercise. Then close the book (and your eyes) and focus on your fingers. If you have to read all exercises, this chapter will be a pain in the "@#%*$@$@"!

TIP!! To get the most out of these exercises, "bang" the valves down so shifting between notes becomes so destinct as possible.

© 2012 Improve Your Game - JGMusik ApS DK

Expand to two octaves. Remember - 3 strikes and you're out!!

Take a well-deserved break. Then play something beautiful.

If you're a practice geek - you write Level 4! :-)

Dexterity Exercises -level 3

Still long and boring. But necessary. So on to quintuplets.

In Exercise 9 we expand to two octaves. Remember - if you don't get it in three attempts - you're out. Eventually you will succeed - I promise!!

Do yourself a favor. Thoroughly understand the concept of each exercise. Then close the book (and your eyes) and focus on your fingers. If you have to read all exercises, this chapter will be a real pain in the tukos.

Spread the different groupings over your week or just take 2-3 each day, so you don't get crazy. 1/8 triplets monday, 1/16 tuesday etc..

TIP!! To get the most out of these exercises "bang" the valves down so shift between notes becomes so destinct as possible.

Expand to two octaves. Remember - ***3 strikes and you're out!***

WISE TRUMPET TAPAS - "PRACTISE"

- Strive to reach complete technical liberation and enter the sphere of music

- Practise in short spurts. Focus on a few bars or a reduced passage

- Practise intervals slowly until you strike each note directly in its center

- Practise all technical material musically

- Practise Eb music on Bb-trumpet.

- Do something else to fill the space while you are resting - internet for instance :-)

- When practising, make sure the rhythm begins on the first beat - not after.

- Read an upper register passage down an octave to develop ease and security

- Finish with soft playing to fine tune the aperture.

- Lean into the horn.

By Jan Glaesel

The Complete Method For Trumpet

IMPROVE YOUR GAME

TONGUING - TARGETPRACTICE
PRECISION & ENDURANCE
COLLECTION

Volume IV

WRITTEN BY: JAN GLAESEL
COPYRIGHT © 2012:
JAN GLAESEL / JGMUSIK APS DK
WWW.TRUMPETGAME.COM

JON GORRIE:

In the following chapter on performance - "Just Another Day At The Office" - you are going to meet Jon Gorrie. Jon has been a great help to me in finalizing Improve Your Game.

Jon is a professional trumpet player, brass pedagogue, composer/arranger, and conductor. He is also a performance psychology specialist and author of Performing in The Zone – Unleash your true performing potential!

Originally from New Zealand Jon emigrated in 2003 to Sweden for professional development studies at the Swedish National Orchestra Academy. During this time he was working as a trumpet player with both the Gothenburg Symphony and Gothenburg Opera orchestras.

Since the release of Performing in The Zone in July 2009, Jon has coached private clients and given lectures about performance psychology.

Also well-versed in the relatively new "Print On Demand" publishing technology, Jon presents lectures on this subject and it was at one of these lectures here in Copenhagen in 2011 that I met him. His knowledge came at the exact right time to help me get on and finalize Improve Your Game.

Being a fellow trumpet player we connected instantly, and I got hold of his book, read it, and am excited that Jon has agreed to "lend" me the following article. This will give you a taste of Jon's expertise, and I can only recommend that you pick up a copy of Performing in The Zone yourself and benefit from Jon's knowledge.

YOU CAN PURCHASE THE BOOK AT: WWW.THEZONEBOOK.COM

JUST ANOTHER DAY AT THE OFFICE

How to get better results in concerts, auditions and other high-pressure performing situations" was originally written for classical musicians as an aid in preparing for auditions and other solo performances. However, the information in this article can be applied to anyone in a 'high-pressure' performance situation.

INTRODUCTION

Concerts, auditions, and solo performances – these are generally considered 'under the spotlight' events, and can be experienced by many student performers, adult beginners, and even professionals, with high levels of performance arousal.

"PERFORMANCE AROUSAL? WHAT'S THAT?"

You've no doubt heard about or even experienced feelings of anxiety before or during performances. This anxiety, stage fright, or performance anxiety as it is commonly referred to, is a negative form of performance arousal, and can affect you negatively in performing situations. Excitement on the other hand, or the feeling of looking forward to a performance, is a positive form of performance arousal, and can have a positive effect on your ability to perform, if the level of excitement you experience is appropriate for your particular performing situation.

However if the level of excitement you experience is inappropriate (i.e. too much or too little) for your performing situation, then this excitement will have a negative effect on your ability to perform. So in short, the term "performance arousal" describes the excitement or anxiety you may feel before or during performances. It can be a hindrance, or a help, and can be felt particularly strongly in 'under the spotlight' events, or other performing situations that you perceive as 'high-pressure'.

"OK. SO HOW MUCH POSITIVE PERFORMANCE AROUSAL (EXCITEMENT) DO I NEED TO GET THE BEST RESULTS WHEN I'M PERFORMING."

As a musician performing in a concert, recital, or audition situation, high levels of excitement may make you feel like you are shaky and out of control. Likewise, performance anxiety can also make you feel out of control, and in addition may be accompanied by unpleasant physical sensations such as muscular tension, hyperventilation, sweaty palms, nausea, and so on. So, in traditional concert, recital, or audition situations, a moderately low level of positive performance arousal (excitement) will in most cases allow you to achieve your best possible results.

"THAT SOUNDS LIKE IT SHOULD WORK IN THEORY. BUT HOW DO I ACTUALLY MAKE IT HAPPEN?"

In this article you'll be shown the simple yet powerful technique of Intense Positive Visualisation. This technique has been specifically designed to help you obtain an ideal state of mind for your performing situations, regardless of your field of performance. Using Intense Positive Visualisation, you can achieve better results in concerts and auditions, and see how other 'high-pressure' performance situations may be perceived as easy, comfortable, and dare I say, even a joy to experience!

FAMILIARITY

To begin with, let's take a situation quite apart from a musical one. Let's imagine for a minute that you are an office worker beginning your first day at a new job. As with a recital or audition, this is a situation that can put you in the stressful position of not knowing exactly what will happen throughout the course of the experience. You might have a certain amount of information, but there are still many variables and details that are either unfamiliar, or completely unknown. You are also quite naturally aware that the outcome of the actual event is significant, especially given the importance placed on first impressions.

WHAT ARE SOME OF THE PHYSICAL AND MENTAL RESPONSES THAT YOU MIGHT EXPERIENCE BEFORE AND/OR DURING YOUR 'EVER-IMPORTANT' FIRST DAY AT THE OFFICE?

Perhaps you might have sweaty palms, shallow breathing, a churning stomach, or possibly mixed feelings of excitement and anxiety. However, after experiencing your new environment for a few days, you begin to perceive being at the office as no big deal. When this happens, the heightened excitement or anxiety (performance arousal) you experienced on your first day starts to disappear.

> Now, compare the number of times you've heard of the phrase:
> **I'M STARTING MY NEW JOB TODAY. WISH ME LUCK!**
>
> with the phrase:
> **IT'S MY 30TH DAY AT THE OFFICE TODAY. WISH ME LUCK!**
>
> and not to mention:
> **IT'S MY 2,623RD DAY AT THE OFFICE TODAY. WISH ME LUCK!**
>
> It starts to sound ridiculous, doesn't it? So therefore, and this really is the crux of the matter, what is the difference between the ever so slightly ridiculous sounding 2,623rd day at the office and the 1st day at the office?

The answer is familiarity! And it is a special sort of familiarity that helps us feel at ease, calm, confident and in control. This sort of familiarity can be referred to as positive conditioning.

RIDING THE ROLLER COASTER!!

To explain positive conditioning in plain English, picture this… You are at a theme park and are very nervous or anxious about riding that big, scary roller coaster for the first time. Even thinking about taking the plunge starts you off on a serious emotional roller coaster!

SHOULD I? SHOULDN'T I? I DON'T REALLY WANT TO AFTER ALL. BUT I DO WANT TO TRY IT, AND ALL MY FRIENDS ARE DOING IT. I CAN DO IT. I CAN'T DO IT. IT MIGHT BE FUN!? BUT WHAT HAPPENS IF WE CRASH? MAYBE I SHOULD HAVE JUST STAYED IN BED THIS MORNING!

Eventually you decide to board the roller coaster, and experience the ride. Riding the roller coaster turns out to be a positive experience – you survived and even enjoyed it in some weird way! This makes your brain suddenly say, "Hey! That wasn't so bad after all!" The next time you think about riding the roller coaster, you are perhaps only a little nervous or anxious.

You make the decision to ride the roller coaster again, and again it turns out to be a positive experience – you even had your eyes open this time! Your brain now says to you, "Hey! That was actually kinda fun! I wanna do it again!" And so the next time you think about riding the roller coaster, you are looking forward to it, because you know it will be a fun, enjoyable experience! This is how positive conditioning works.

However, what if your experiences are negative? For example, what happens if the first time you ride the roller coaster you get stuck at the top of the ride and are forced to dangle upside-down for 6 hours because of a technical problem? If this happens, your brain is probably going to say to you the next time you think about riding a roller coaster, "Oi! Remember that last roller coaster experience?? It was horrible! I don't ever want to go through that again – get me outta here!" This is negative conditioning in action.

KEEP READING TO FIND OUT HOW POSITIVE CONDITIONING CAN HELP YOU!

"THE ROUTINE - PART 1

So, how do we ensure your brain tells you that auditions, recitals, and other 'high-pressure' performing situations are easy and fun? How do you achieve positive conditioning when you only get one shot at something??? We'll answer these questions very soon! But for now, it's back to the office! After 30 days at the office, you know the routine…

- Wake up with the alarm clock, hit the 'snooze' button, and sleep for an extra 10 minutes
- Get out of bed when the alarm rings for the second time
- Eat breakfast
- Have a shower and get dressed
- Brush teeth
- Shoes on
- Leave the house after locking the door
- Walk to the bus stop. Aim to arrive there in time to get on the number 85 bus that you know always leaves 2 or 3 minutes earlier than it's supposed to
- Board the bus
- Get off the bus at the appropriate stop

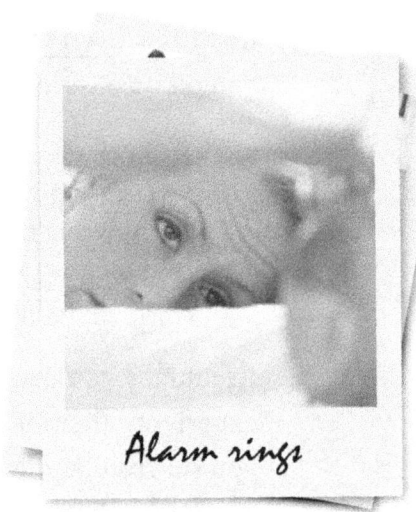

Alarm rings

"THE ROUTINE - PART 2 A

- Greet the receptionist
- Sign in
- Walk up the stairs, bidding a fellow colleague a good day on the way
- Greet the other office workers as you pass them on your way to your desk
- Arrive at your desk, sit down, and start the day's work
- Lunch break for 45 minutes
- Work through to the late afternoon
- When it's time to leave, walk back down the stairs, out of the office, and out of the building.

All of these small but necessary actions are completed each day as part of your routine. Thinking back to your first day at the office, you didn't have this routine – your first day was completely unfamiliar! This is the reason why you may have been feeling anxious or even overexcited (high performance arousal level), and the reason why you asked your partner, flatmate, friends, or family to "wish you luck."

Now, if it feels like we have wandered from the path of an 'under the spotlight' performance situation, read the bullet points in "The Routine" – Part 1 again, and then skip directly to "The Routine" – Part 2 B below.

"THE ROUTINE - PART 2 B

- Walk around to the stage door of the venue.
- Greet the receptionist at the desk.
- Sign in.
- Walk up the stairs and along the corridor to warm-up room marked 'Soloist 1'.
- Take out your instrument, and begin your warm-up routine.
- After some time, your accompanist enters the warm-up room.
- With 15 minutes until your audition is scheduled to start, you rehearse entries and certain problem passages.
- The stage manager knocks on the door, and asks if you are both ready.
- You follow the stage manager to the wings in the off-stage area.
- You walk confidently on stage, with your accompanist following closely behind.
- You acknowledge the audition jury.
- You begin the audition calmly, and confidently.
- The performance begins, and continues in the most musical way you can possibly imagine.
- You finish the last audition piece, acknowledge the jury, and finally walk off stage.

So, if you're a performer, and get the chance to be 'at the office' for 30 days (performing in recitals or auditions every day for 30 days) you can get to know the routine, and become quite comfortable and familiar with it.

BUT WAIT A SECOND! YOU MIGHT BE THINKING:

"Ok, but the office worker has the opportunity to learn the routine and get familiar with it as they are in reality at the office every weekday. I'm not doing a recital or audition everyday. I only get one shot at this!
What???
You're right! You're not performing in a recital or audition everyday, but you should be!
What? Auditions and recitals don't come along everyday!
In reality, no they don't! But in your mind, you can perform auditions and recitals as often as you wish!

WHAT DO YOU MEAN?!? HOW DOES THIS WORK?

By using specially designed visualisation techniques, you can use your mind to rehearse any 'one-shot' performance as many times as you wish! Therefore, you can become familiar with your 'one-shot' performing situation, well before it even happens!

So, if you practise visualisation techniques, when you walk into your performing situation in reality, you're just like the office worker going to work on their 30th or even 2,623rd day at the office! In other words, you can feel, calm, confident, and in control in any performance situation!

THE PROOF

"But wait just another second! Surely there is a vast difference between experiencing an event in reality and experiencing the same event in your imagination? After all, the office worker actually is at the office every day, and if I use visualisation, I'm only going to imagine myself being at 'the office'. Can this really be the same thing?"

The short answer to this question is YES!
According to many studies on visualisation in the field of sports psychology, the subconscious mind doesn't know the difference between actually experiencing an event, and simply imagining an event in vivid detail! Look at this example:

One study on visualisation in sports psychology involved the members of three basketball teams of approximately equal skill level, practising shooting '3-pointers', for a period of 30 days. One of the teams practised neither physically on the court, nor in their minds during the duration of the study. Their improvement at the end of the study was not surprisingly 0%. Another team practised physically – that is, on the basketball court – for a period of one hour each day. After 30 days, their improvement was measured at 24%. The third team did not practise physically at all but was told to mentally visualise the game for one hour each day. At the end of the thirty day period, their improvement was a remarkable 23%.

WHAT WAS THE REASON FOR THIS?

The sports scientists concluded that the subconscious mind cannot differentiate between what is real and what is imagined. Therefore, since the subconscious mind has a large influence on how you perform, positively conditioning your subconscious mind using Intense Positive Visualisation can have a huge effect on your success as a performer! Keep reading to find out about Intense Positive Visualisation!

INTENSE POSITIVE VISUALIZATION

Visualization techniques can help you positively condition yourself to achieve an ideal state of mind, helping you to gain optimal results in your performing situations. In short, when visualising, you train your mind by entering a relaxed state and imagining the exact results you would like to achieve. By regularly practising visualisation techniques, you can condition yourself for success!

In the book "Performing in The Zone", three different types of visualisation techniques are explained:

- **SNAP SHOT**
- **INTENSE POSITIVE VISUALIZATION**
- **THE 5 SENSE VISUALIZATION METHOD**

Here in "Just Another Day at the Office" you're going to see exactly how the simple yet powerful technique of Intense Positive Visualization can help you in your performing situations! Read on!

DIFFERENT POINTS OF VIEW

Intense Positive Visualization can be carried out in the 1st person or 3rd person perspective. Using the 1st person perspective, you put yourself in the centre of the visualization. For example, if you are a concert pianist, you would imagine yourself performing on stage from your own eyes, seeing your hands and the piano keyboard in front of you, taking in the experience as if you were actually carrying it out in reality.

In the 3rd person perspective, you would see yourself from a distance, possibly from a seat in the audience, the back of the room, or even a position up in the ceiling somewhere above, behind, or beside you.

Some performers find a 1st person visualization to be more powerful and real, whereas others may find a 3rd person visualisation to be most effective. Experiment using both viewpoints, and discover which one works best for you.

INTENSE POSITIVE VISUALIZATION EXPLAINED

To practise Intense Positive Visualisation, you will need to be undisturbed for a period of anywhere from ten minutes to an hour, depending on the length of the performance you are about to visualise.

Intense Positive Visualization is best carried out lying down on your back with your hands resting gently on your solar-plexus. You may choose to lie flat on the floor or on a yoga mattress. Lying down on a bed can be an acceptable alternative, and is at times preferable if practising this exercise just before sleeping. It's important to keep the body at a comfortable temperature throughout the duration of the visualization, and therefore covering yourself with a blanket might be necessary.

To begin Intense Positive Visualization, gently close your eyes, and lightly touch your tongue to the front part of the roof of your mouth, just behind the teeth. This is a Qi Gong technique which forms an 'energy bridge' to allow freer flow of energy in the human energy system. Try to keep the root of your tongue relaxed at all times. If you have trouble with this, simply let your tongue sit in its natural position and come back to this Qi Gong energy bridge technique at a later stage. Whilst in a horizontal position, allow the floor to take your weight. Feel your limbs becoming heavier the more relaxed they feel.

Trust the floor – it will hold you. Give in to the support from underneath. Trust, relax, and let go.

Breathe gently through your nose. Allow your body to breathe as it needs to.

The next part of "Just another day at the office…" is designed to help you understand how Intense Positive Visualization works. It is an example of one possible visualization, taken from the perspective of a musician giving a recital, requiring a performance arousal level of +1 before the performance, +2 for the majority of the recital, and +3 for the climax of the concert.

After reading the example and understanding the process of Intense Positive Visualization explained below, you can then create your own personal visualisation to meet your specific needs. When creating your visualization, remember to visualise events exactly as you want them to be.

KEEP READING FOR AN EXAMPLE OF INTENSE POSITIVE VISUALISATION!

START OF INTENSE POSITIVE VISUALISATION - EXAMPLE:

You begin by imagining yourself at home, taking your performance clothes out of the wardrobe. You check to see that everything is in order with your clothes and your performance shoes. You put your performance clothes and shoes in a suit bag, pick up your instrument case, check to see if you have your keys and wallet, and leave the house, locking the door behind you. You walk down the stairs and out on to the street in a relaxed pace. Arriving at the metro (underground train/'tube') station, you use your ticket to pass the barrier, and board your train. It's going to be a great show. Your performance arousal level is at +1. You feel relaxed, positive, and calm.

Getting off at the right stop, you stroll towards the recital hall, taking in the scenery on the way. Perhaps a seagull is calling in the distance? How do the trees look? Are there other people out walking? You take out your Cue Card and slowly read over your key words. Your performance arousal level is at +1. You feel relaxed, positive, and calm.

You arrive at the venue and greet the receptionist on the way in. After signing in, you head to your warm up room where your accompanist is already waiting for you. You ask your accompanist for 15 minutes by yourself so that you can prepare yourself and warm up. You unpack your instrument, and begin your warm up routine. It feels fantastic to start warming up. You know your accompanist is going help you put on a great show. You know that the venue has a warm acoustic.

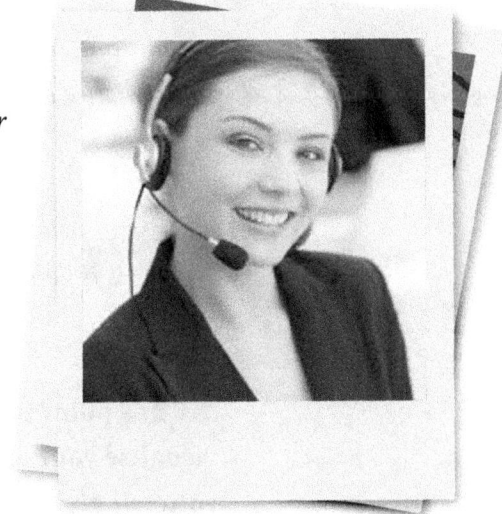

Your performance clothes are ironed and your shoes polished. You are ready. You are about to share part of yourself with some people who want to hear you – they want to be touched by you. It's going to be a warm, giving, rewarding experience for both them and you. It's going to be great! Your performance arousal level is at +1. You feel relaxed, positive, and calm.

After 15 minutes your accompanist walks in to the room. Before you begin to rehearse, you check your Cue Card again, and go through your Pre-Performance Ritual, "C3" – calm, controlled, confident – the "C3" and "+1" on your Cue Card gives you a familiar, friendly reminder. (Cue Cards, Pre-Performance Rituals, and "C3" are explained in "Performing in The Zone")

You rehearse the beginning of the first piece with your accompanist. It's easy and free. The acoustic in the practise room is dry, but you know that out there in the hall the space will take care of you – the warm reverb will beautify every nuance and add to the experience for everyone.

Your performance arousal level is at +1. You feel relaxed, positive, and calm. When it is time, you are called to the wings of the stage. You take one final look at your Cue Card and go through the "C3" exercise again. You can hear the chatter of the audience, and see the stage in front of you. You walk calmly, securely, and with purpose on to the stage where you are greeted by applause. They like you and you haven't even done anything yet! This is going to be a fun performance! Your performance arousal level is at +1. You feel relaxed, positive, and calm.
Whilst your accompanist adjusts the piano stool, you look out into the audience and make visual contact with the people you are about to touch with your performance.
Your body language exudes confidence and assuredness. You greet the audience, introducing yourself and your accompanist, and begin to talk about the evening's programme. Your voice is stable, powerful, and reflects the perfect +1 state of performance arousal that you are currently in. Your voice resonates effortlessly to the back of the hall. You are in The Zone.

After your brief introductory talk, you look to your accompanist who is ready to work with you. This is going great! You begin your performance, and your performance arousal gently rises to a +2.

"At this point in the visualisation I strongly suggest that you visualise your entire performance – that is, see and hear yourself giving the most musical, fantastic, controlled, inspired, moving performance you can possibly imagine. Use either 1st or 3rd person perspective. In your visualisation you are doing everything right – it feels fantastic and sounds amazing. You are at an ideal level of performance arousal for this performing situation, and totally in The Zone."

Just before the climax of the final piece, you turn the page, and see the familiar figure of "+3" that you wrote earlier at the top of your music. You step it up a notch, and raise your performance arousal level to +3. The music takes on a new life and energy and this is felt by you, your accompanist, and the audience. Finishing the concert at a +3 level your audience erupts in cheers and applause. You did it! It was great!! You were in The Zone! You acknowledge the audience, and walk off stage.

END OF INTENSE POSITIVE VISUALISATION EXAMPLE

When you feel ready, slowly begin to move your body again. How did it feel to give that amazing performance? You were great! Everything just 'clicked'. You were totally and completely in The Zone throughout the entire process. Intense Positive Visualisation can be practised every day before a performance. By doing so, you can condition yourself to perform in The Zone. Intense Positive Visualisation is highly recommended to all performers about to give important performances, auditions or recitals.

The earlier you begin Intense Positive Visualisation the better, but at least one week prior to the performance event should be the minimum.

In your own visualisations, remember to assess how much positive performance arousal you need at various moments: +1, +2, +3, +4, or +5. Do you need to be at the same activation level for the entire event, or does your performance arousal level need to modulate at various times? Remember that imagining yourself calm and relaxed probably isn't going to give you the best results if you are preparing for an intensely physical, fast-paced performance situation. Likewise, visualising getting yourself psyched up and exploding out of the gates isn't going to help you if you are preparing for a more delicate +1 situation, such as a slow movement of a concerto.

VISUALISING PERFORMING WITH AN IDEAL LEVEL OF PERFORMANCE AROUSAL IS IMPORTANT!

By using Intense Positive Visualisation, you are using positive conditioning to become familiar with as many elements of your performance day as possible, and become used to experiencing these always in a positive light.

Notice also that Intense Positive Visualisation goes into as much detail as possible, both before and during your performance. This is to help take away as many surprises and unknown factors on the day of your performance as possible.

It may help the accuracy and intensity of your visualisation to do some reconnaissance by actually visiting the performance venue prior to your performance event. This is easily possible for students giving final recitals for example, or sportspeople playing at a local venue.

Try to also incorporate some variations in your visualisations. Perhaps the audience isn't ready and takes an extra 5 minutes to get seated? Perhaps your accompanist arrives later than expected due to traffic problems? Maybe the stage curtains are blue and not red? Perhaps the warm up room is bigger or smaller? Regardless of what happens, you are prepared, and you stay in your ideal level of positive performance arousal. You are completely stable, and in The Zone, always.

"BY USING INTENSE POSITIVE VISUALISATION EVERY DAY OVER A PERIOD OF ONE WEEK, YOU HAVE IN EFFECT CARRIED OUT YOUR PERFORMANCE SUCCESSFULLY 7 TIMES. PRACTISE THIS VISUALISATION 3 TIMES PER DAY FOR A WEEK AND YOU'VE COMPLETED 21 SUCCESSFUL, POSITIVE, GREAT, FANTASTIC, EASY, IDEAL PERFORMANCES, AND HAVE BEEN IN THE ZONE EVERY SINGLE TIME!"

Remember that your subconscious doesn't differentiate between what is real and what is imagined. Therefore by using Intense Positive Visualisation diligently, you are conditioning yourself for success by becoming familiar with performing in The Zone!

By using the technique of Intense Positive Visualisation, you can experience your next audition, recital or 'high-pressure' performance as just another day at the office!

JAN GLAESEL:
"I URGE YOU TO READ JONS ENTIRE BOOK "PERFORMING IN THE ZONE". YOU CAN ORDER IT AT":

WWW.THEZONEBOOK.COM

WISE TRUMPET TAPAS - "TONGUING"

- Match single- and double tonguing.
- Practise tonguing slowly - then gradually add speed.
- Use single tonguing unless absolutely necessary. This increases your chances of accuracy and cleanliness.
- Bring the tongue forward, towards the back of the upper teeth to avoid heavy staccato.
- Use minimum tongue movement - no more than needed
- The tongue is the valve. It's important to penetrate the column of air but not to upset or shatter it.
- Move air, even when tonguing
- The only weapon that becomes sharper with constant use - is the tongue.
- Master single tonguing before approaching multiple tonguing
- Tongue clearly when playing soft.
- Relax in your throat when tonguing.

This is the DNA of trumpet playing

Single -Tonguing/Attack

I play these exercises daily to keep focus and to check up on my tonguing. I've never been satisfied with my own tonguing, even down to my single note-attack. Here is why. Your tongues movement ALWAYS has to be fast and with the smallest amplitude possible. My mistake was that I always changed either the size or speed of movement, depending whether I played long, short, loud or soft tones.

These exercises focus on even tonguing no matter what you're playing.

Listen to your attacks. They should be as clean and identical as possible. Aim for no leakage of air before the sound of the tone. I can explain the difference with the two consonants "T" and "S". If you say "T", there is no sound before the "T", BUT if you say "S" there I actually an long "E" before the "S" – THAT'S THE DIFFERENCE!!. Your focus should be on "T" when practicing single-tonguing.

Repeats in Exercise 1 are open – repeat until attacks are clean and identical.

Exercise 1 is quite simple. You start with the root in the first two bars, followed by going down to the 5th and then walks back to the root. I've chosen "C" as my root, but feel free to take it in any key you wish – middle "C" is just easy. An octave up or down does makes it harder – but it's good practice.

Exercise 2 starts on th 5th and you then walks down to the root. There are three versions of this exercise - 1/4-notes, 1/8-notes and 1/16-notes. Each are played legato, tenuto, and staccato.
I chose G major, but as a challenge, take it in any key you wish.

The first notes one in each grouping is slurred to show you how it's supposed to sound when you start tonguing it.

Still focus on a clean and identical attack even though the rhythm changes. Choose your own tempo but don't play it so fast that your attacks aren't clean and identical.

Mastering this makes life a whole lot easier

Focus On Attack Exercise

(Please read introduction to chapter for reference)

♩ = your choice

© 2012 Improve Your Game - JGMusik ApS DK

simile......

simile......

simile......

simile......

simile......

simile......

simile......

© 2012 Improve Your Game - JGMusik ApS DK

Show me what you got!

Single Tonguing Etude

Jan Glaesel

Now we're going to do some tongue twisting :-)

Double Tounging - Level 1

Double tonguing is a pain in the &!%!!. Since my days in the Tivoli Boys Guard I haven't had to use it -or so I thought!! Since I rediscovered my passion for my instrument, I found out that no matter what type of music you play, you can always use double and triple-tonguing.

The first secret behind good tonguing is to relax in the throat. The second secret is to even out the sound between the T and the K articulations. The third secret is to start slowly and then gradually play the exercises faster to get your tonguing, fingers, throat and brain to work together. Oh yeah, try to relax at the same time.

Exercises 1 and 2 should also be practiced according to variations below. In the beginning it will sound poorly.

© 2012 Improve Your Game - JGMusik ApS DK

Instead of jumping directly from the key of C in Exercise 1, to G in Exercise 2 feel free to play the same exercise in the keys of Db, D, Eb, E, F and F#.

Exercise 3 should also be practiced with the following articulation variations:

Exercise 4 should also be practiced with the following articulation variations:

Double-Tonguing Etude 1

Jan Glaesel

(Use only double-tounging on 1/16-notes)

♩ = 120

Allegro Moderato

© 2012 Improve Your Game - JGMusik ApS DK

Just to make you feel better - I suck at this! Big time!!!!!!

Double-Tonguing Level 2 - The Need For Speed!!

The rhythmic pattern in Exercise 1 is the foundation for the following studies. Learn it by heart and you can practice it while walking, driving, etc.. You don't need a trumpet for that. The more familiar you are with the pattern, the more relaxed your throat will be - thats what we're looking for. Aim for as little tongue movement as possible.

Start playing the exercise on G. When you're more relaxed you can move up chromatically. Don't move it or change tempo before you're comfortable with where you are.

Same rhythmic pattern as in Exercise 1, but now we start moving the fingers :-)

© 2012 Improve Your Game - JGMusik ApS DK

311

Diatonic Melody Versions

Chromatic Melody Versions

Interval Melody Versions

316

Double-Tonguing Etude 2

Jan Glaesel

WISE TRUMPET TAPAS - "PLAYING"

- Slur everything first, then add articulations

- Strive for a balanced embouchure where the workload is evenly distributed

- When performing "hear" the music - leave the technical concerns in the practise room.

- Playing the entire piece may overtax the chops. Save it for the performance.

- When slurring down, think of the same (upper) note twice

- Use the word "simple" to set the embouchure - freeze on the "m" and there you have it!!

- The less effort, the better the sound.

- Trust that playing can be easy.

- Squeeze as much music as you can out of the lyrical studies.

- When slurring up, blow into the lower note before moving.

© 2012 Improve Your Game - JGMusik ApS DK

If your face could get a hernia - this is the way to get it !!

Triple-Tonguing Studies - Level 1

If double-tonguing is a pain in the %&#!!, triple-tonguing is twice the pain. Although its most common use is in classical music, you can use in any style and it's a hell of a way to improve your attack,

These exercises have the same concept as theones from the previous chapter on double-tonguing. Don't start triple-tonguing before you have a good grip on your double-tonguing. Same rules applies here as in the chapter on double-tonguing.

Exercises 1 and 2 should also be practiced according to variations below:

Instead of jumping directly an octave up, play Exercise 1 chromaticly up from D to D.
Start slowly and then gradually play the exercises faster to get your tongue, fingers, throat and brain working together - and try to relax at the same time.

© 2012 Improve Your Game - JGMusik ApS DK

When you feel that you are ready, Exercise 3 should be practiced with these two variations in the diferent keys:

Triple-Tonguing Level 2 - The Need For Even More Speed!

As in the chapter on double-tonguing, the rhythmic pattern in Exercise 1 is the foundation for the following studies. Learn it by heart and you can practice it while walking, driving, etc.. You don't need a trumpet for that. The more familiar you are with the pattern, the more relaxed your throat will be - thats what we're looking for. Aim for as little tongue movement as possible.

Start playing the exercise on G. When you're more relaxed you can move up chromatically. Don't move it or change tempo before you're comfortable with where you are.

Same rhythmic pattern as in Exercise 1, but now we start moving the fingers :-)

Triple-Tonguing - Scale Versions

Triple-Tonguing - Chromatic Versions

Triple Tonguing - Interval Versions

Put on a happy face and have some fun with this.
Triple Tonguing - Slapstick Etude
Jan Glaesel

© 2012 Improve Your Game - JGMusik ApS DK

Even if your tongue is not broken by now, it still needs some rest. :)

Are you a Man??......... or a Mouse?? We will see..........

Target Practice - Endurance Level 1

In trumpet playing, it has always been a very high goal to hit the notes - dead on. Unlike many other instruments, the trumpet is an instrument that can't hide in a section. If a trumpet player plays a wrong note, he can easily overpower a string section of 40 players. That is why you must be accurate.

These exercises are for adjusting your ai, and to give you the self-confidence needed to hit any note - no matter what the range.

You should be able to play at least two of the exercises, 1-2, 2-3, 3-4 or 4-5. Remember - don't force it. Make only three attempts. *3 strikes and you're out.* Be patient - all good things will come to those who wait.

Play all exercises with a full sound about forte. As you ascend, use the dynamic level necessary.

TIP 1 - Only play one of the Target Practice Levels Studies each day. (1, 2 or 3)

TIP 2 - When playing in a band, if you play a wrong note - just look at the guy next to you while shaking your head. Works every time! :-)

© 2012 Improve Your Game - JGMusik ApS DK

Man or mouse?? Can't tell yet? Then you need more practice!

Target Practice - Endurance Level 2

The objective is the same but the octaves and directions are changing twice during each staff.
Try to lock your embouchure and adjust by tightening in the high octaves and relaxing in the low ones.
This and accelerating the airstream, should do the trick.

Remember - *3 strikes and you are out!!*

Is it a bird? - Is it a plane??

Targetpractice - Endurance Level 3

Still the same objective but now accelerating the airstream is everything.

Remember: *3 Strikes and you're out!!*

338

Bird? Plane? No! - It's Superman!!! Good job!!

© 2012 Improve Your Game - JGMusik ApS DK

This is some scary stuff!!

Becoming A Marksman - Level 1

As a lead player your worst nightmare is drastic change of dynamics. It's one thing to hit notes at triple forte but a totally different ballgame to go from playing loud to suddenly playing very soft. And if you have to change register on top of that, it takes really good technique to master that.

Malcolm McNab once told me that his work as a trumpet player in the movie business in L.A. is 90 % sheer boredom and 10 % absolute terror. When those guys show up for work, they dont know what they are going to play - so they have to be prepared for anything. The next couple of exercises - Becoming A Marksman and "Get Rid of the Terror, Levels 1,2 and 3 - helps you to master that feeling of terror.

As in many other aspects of performing, a simple rule applies here - the more you practice the hard stuff, the better you will become at it. Eventually your fear of failure will disappear. Simple as that.

Remember - dont push it!! *3 strikes and you are out.*

© 2012 Improve Your Game - JGMusik ApS DK

Cool down phrase

Take A 10 Minute Break

Get Rid Of The Terror - Level 1

Get Rid Of The Terror - Level 2

Get Rid Of The Terror - Level 3

Before taking a small break - play this cool down phrase

Cool down phrase

© 2012 Improve Your Game - JGMusik ApS DK

Finally - some real music. Thank you!!

Lyrical Etudes - Level 1

Please read note two pages ahead in the end of this level

Jan Glaesel

Jan Glaesel

Jan Glaesel

© 2012 Improve Your Game - JGMusik ApS DK

Jan Glaesel

I just love to play melodic/lyrical music. These small pieces of music are inspired by the Arban method. As a kid in The Tivoli Boys Guard it actually hated to practise. The only thing that kept me going, was that, in the back of the Arban, were a collection of small pieces of music ranging from folk songs to small cadenzas and themes from more or less well know operas.

True Story:
Actually I hated so much practesing, that I recorded some exercises, studies and other stuff from Arban on my fathers tape-recorder and played them in my room, while reading Donald Duck cartoons in my bed (sorry Mum & Dad). I had a note stuck on my door saying: **"Don't disturb - I'm pratesing"**

I also used a lot of Music Minus One, a brand new concept in the 70th. - that made sense to me. Again it had to do with actually playing music with a purpose. Thats why I've tried to put so much music as possible into these 4 volumes.

Hope you like it!!

P.S. In this chapter and the rest of this volume I collected all the musical treats that I spread around in the other 3 volumes for your convenience - and some extra bonus pieces. Enjoy.

Lyrical Etudes - Level 2

Jan Glaesel

Allegro Vivace

Jan Glaesel

Andante cantabile

Waltz For Trumpet

Jan Glaesel

My First Etude For Trumpet - F major

Jan Glaesel

Etude Picturesque - E minor

Jan Glaesel

Single-Tonguing Etude

Jan Glaesel

Double-Tonguing Etude 1

(Use only double-tonguing o 1/16-notes)

Jan Glaesel

© 2012 Improve Your Game - JGMusik ApS DK

Trumpet Menuet Etude - D minor

Jan Glaesel

Playful Trumpet Etude - A major

Jan Glaesel

Dedicated to my good friend and trumpet player Gary Cordell in Las Vegas Nevada

Etude for A Friend - C minor

Jan Glaesel

Now that I've finished this book - I want to go home

Yearning For Home

Jan Glaesel

Hate myself for writing this!!
Opt.

To a new friend, wonderful trumpet player and great inspiration - Jon Gorrie

Etude Ritmico Spiccato - A major
Use double tounguing where necessary

Jan Glaesel

Double-Tonguing Etude 2

Jan Glaesel

Put on a happy face and have some fun with this
Triple-Tonguing - Slapstick Etude

Jan Glaesel

Dedicated to Nikolaj Viltoft - friend and trumpet player for the Royal Danish Opera

Etude For A Mentor - Eb major

Jan Glaesel

Vivace con spirituoso

© 2012 Improve Your Game - JGMusik ApS DK

Before we go completely Maurice André - let's blow of some steam! Dedicated to my friend Tony Scodwell

Latin Jazz Etude
Try playing this one with a rhythm section!

Jan Glaesel

WISE TRUMPET TAPAS - "PLAYING"

- Endurance difficulties are usually due to tension in the breath

- Sing and finger the passage you just completed while you rest

- Play into the center of notes, think down. The center of notes are lower than you think.

- Always commence with a clean attack and centre.

- **Nothing is so high that it can't be played an octave or two lower.**

- When performing, "hear" the music. leave the technical concerns in the practice room.

- Hear the pitch before playing any note.

- Keep throat open. Keep tongue down.

- Slur everything first, then add articulations.

- Nothing is so fast that it can't be played slower.

- Exaggerate dynamics.

© 2012 Improve Your Game - JGMusik ApS DK

Dedicated to trumpet player Per Nielsen

Etude Melancolico

Jan Glæsel

© 2012 Improve Your Game - JGMusik ApS DK

Dedicated to Malcolm McNab - trumpet virtuoso

Lyrical Interval Etude

Jan Glaesel

Rubato   Molto Espressivo

© 2012 Improve Your Game - JGMusik ApS DK

Trumpets Incorporated

Dedicated to all the crazy trumpet players in the world.

Jan Glaesel

Trumpets Incoporated

Trumpets Incoporated

Trumpets Incoporated

Trumpets Incoporated

Trumpets Incoporated

Trumpets Incoporated

Trumpets Incoporated
Solo Trumpet

387

© 2012 Improve Your Game - JGMusik ApS DK

III Trumpet

Trumpets Incorporated

Dedicated to all the crazy trumpet players in the world.

Jan Glaesel

Trumpets Incoporated
IV Trumpet

Trumpets Incorporated

Dedicated to all the crazy trumpet players in the world.

Jan Glaesel

© 2012 Improve Your Game - JGMusik ApS DK

MY BOOKSHELF OF CONSTANT INSPIRATION

When I started to practice for real in 2004 the only method-book I had was:

J.S. ARBAN - COMPLETE CONSERVATORY METHOD FOR TRUMPET

This was the book I was handed back in 1967 when I join the Tivoli Boys Guard here in Copenhagen. I think it is considered one of the "bibles" for many trumpet players. In 2004 when I began my new journey I started collecting all kinds of trumpet method books. Here is a list of the content of "My bookshelf of constant inspiration", in random order.

Author	Title	Publisher
J.B. Arban	Complete Conservatory Method for Trumpet	Carl Fischer
Herbert L. Clarke	Technical Studies for the Cornet	Carl Fischer
Arturo Sandoval	Playing techniques & Performance Studies Vol. 1-3	Hal Leonard
James Stamp	Warm-Ups & Studies	Editions BIM
Claude Gordon	Systematic Approach to Daily Practice	Carl Fischer
Allen Vizzutti	The Allen Vizzutti Trumpet Method Vol. 1-3	Alfred Publishing
Geoff Winstead	The Real Way to Play the Cat Anderson Method	GWM Publishing
Carmine Caruso	Musical Calisthenics for Brass	Hal Leonard
Max Schlossberg	Daily Drills & Technical Studies for Trumpet	M. Baron Company
Gabriel Parés Parés	Scales for Cornet or Trumpet	Rubank - Hal Leonard
J.L. Small	27 Melodious and Rhythmical Exercises	Carl Fischer
David Vining	Ear training for Trumpet	Carl Fischer
John McNeil	Jazz Trumpet Techniques	Studio P/R
Charles Colin	Advanced Lip Flexibilities Vol. 1-3	Charles Colin Music
Charles Colin	Complete Modern Method for Trumpet or Cornet	Charles Colin Music
Jon Gorrie	High notes, Low Notes and Everything in Between	www.jongorrie.com

I've worked with all of these books and found, through them, inspiration for my own approach to trumpet playing. I pay my deepest respects to all of the writers, and it's with the utmost humility I've used them as inspiration for my version of the ultimate Trumpet Method Book.

MUSICAL STUDIES & ETUDES:

Musical studies and etudes are just as important as technical studies. Below you will find some of my favorite collections from my bookshelf. I divide my time between Technical Studies, Musical Studies and Etudes 50/50 - I urge you to do the same.

Author	Title	Publisher
Sigmund Hering	Thirty Etudes for Trumpet or Cornet	Carl Fischer
Sigmund Hering	Thirty-two Etudes for Trumpet or Cornet	Carl Fischer
Sigmund Hering	Forty Progressive Etudes for Trumpet	Carl Fischer
Kopprasch	Sixty Selected Studies for Trumpet	Carl Fischer
H. Voxman	H. Selected Studies for Cornet or Trumpet	Rubank - Hal Leonard
H. Voxman	H. Selected Duets for Cornet or Trumpet Vol. 1-2	Rubank - Hal Leonard
H. Voxman	Concert&Contest Collection for Cornet or Trumpet	Rubank - Hal Leonard
Larry Clark	Progressive Duets for Trumpet in Bb Vol. 1-2	Carl Fischer
Walter Beeler	Solos for the Trumpet-Player	G. Schirmer - Hal Leonard

CREDITS:

Most of all I want, I want thank my loving wife Miriam and the rest of my family for enduring the "awful" sound of practising the trumpet - Thanks guys!!

A special thanks goes to my good friend, and fellow trumpet player **Gary Cordell,** Las Vegas Nevada, for proofreading this project. Also thank you for introducing me to Tony Scodwell.

Tony Scodwell - my good friend and fellow trumpet player, for letting me play one of his fantastic handmade trumpets. "Tony - you're a true artist and craftsman building your fantastic horns."

Bob Reeves - mouthpieces. Thank you for taking almost a day out of your busy schedule to guide me to the mouthpieces which are going to follow me, for the rest of my life.

Jon Gorrie - for opening my eyes to the Print On Demand concept. Also for helping me setting up the whole online marketing side of the project - Let's do something more together.

Krogstrup & Hede - web bureau. For always doing your best for my websites.

Bithiah & Patrick Poulsen - Layout. I love the cover and all your input - thank you.

The Danish Musical Directors Union - for financial support.

Please feel free to contact me with feedback or questions at info@trumpetgame.com

WISE TRUMPET TAPAS - "PLAYING"

Be on time for rehearsals and gigs - that will keep you in business.

Play only as high as you can stay relaxed - otherwise you are practising tension.

Playing situations are rarely ideal. Just enduring the gig and keeping things at the highest level possible, is the name of the game.

When you miss, the problem is not with the "spilt" note, but the one just before it.

Keep the corners of the embouchure anchored and the center flexible

Project your sound as if you are in a concert hall, even when practising.

Don't think of the notes as high. Make them come out easily. Think of them as just another pitch.

Concentrate and focus on attacks and vibrato.

Use "Ah" in all registers

© 2012 Improve Your Game - JGMusik ApS DK

www.ingramcontent.com/pod-product-compliance
Lightning Source LLC
Chambersburg PA
CBHW081344230426

43667CB00017B/2717